SAFETY FIRST
Be safe!

School Safety

STOP

BY SUSAN KESSELRING

ILLUSTRATED BY DAN McGEEHAN

Published by The Child's World®
800-599-READ · childsworld.com

ISBN Information
9781503894006 (Reinforced Library Binding)
9781503895089 (Portable Document Format)
9781503895904 (Online Multi-user eBook)
9781503896727 (Electronic Publication)

LCCN
2024942728

Printed in the United States of America

ABOUT THE AUTHOR

Susan Kesselring loves children, books, nature, and her family. She teaches K-1 students in a progressive charter school down a little country lane in Castle Rock, Minnesota. She is the mother of five daughters and lives in Apple Valley, Minnesota with her husband and a crazy springer spaniel named Lois Lane.

ABOUT THE ILLUSTRATOR

Dan McGeehan spent his younger years as an actor, author, playwright, and editor. Now he spends his days drawing, and he is much happier.

TABLE OF CONTENTS

CHAPTER ONE
School Safety . . . **4**

CHAPTER TWO
Bus Safety . . . **6**

CHAPTER THREE
Walking to School . . . **10**

CHAPTER FOUR
In the Classroom . . . **12**

CHAPTER FIVE
On the Playground . . . **14**

School Safety Rules . . . 20
Wonder More . . . 21
School Safety Hunt . . . 22
Glossary . . . 23
Find Out More . . . 24
Index . . . 24

CHAPTER 1

School Safety

What's the best part of your school day? Is it riding the bus? Maybe it's swinging on the monkey bars at recess. Or do you love solving math problems?

Hi! I'm Buzz B. Safe. Watch for me! I'll show you how to be safe at school.

Being safe at school is an important part of every day.

School is a wonderful place to learn and have fun. But you need to watch out for a few things, too. Learn how to be safe and you will enjoy school even more!

Bus Safety

Hurry, it's time to catch the bus! Ask a parent to walk you to the bus stop and wait with you. Or, walk with friends. It's best to be with someone you know while waiting for the bus.

At your bus stop, watch out for traffic. Remember to stand on the sidewalk. You'll be safer a few feet away from the street.

Can your bus driver see you outside the bus? Make eye contact with your bus driver so you know he or she has seen you. When your bus driver opens the doors, you can climb up the stairs into the bus.

Try to be at the bus stop at least five minutes before your bus is scheduled to arrive.

If you have to walk in front of the bus to get on, stay five big steps from the bus. Stay two big steps away from the sides—except for when you're getting on and off, of course. And never walk behind the bus. Your bus driver cannot see you there.

Once you're on the bus, find a seat right away. Face forward during the ride. Doing so will help keep you safe if there is an **accident**. Keep your feet and school bag out of the middle row where you walk so no one trips. Also, avoid sticking anything out the window. That includes your head and hands!

Your bus driver works hard to get you to school safely. You can help, too. Talk to your friends in a quiet voice. Loud voices can **distract** your bus driver.

Oops! You dropped something by the side of the bus. Just tell your bus driver once you're on your bus. He or she will let you know when it's okay to pick it up.

If you leave something on the bus, do not go back to get it. Ask your bus driver about it the next time you ride the bus.

CHAPTER 3

Walking to School

Do you like walking to school? It's great exercise and fun, too. Make sure you walk with a friend or a parent. If you ride your bike or scooter, wear a helmet.

Rain or snow can make a walk wet or cold, though. What's your plan for walking in bad weather? Ask your parents what to wear and what to do.

Only cross streets where there is a **crosswalk**. Always wait for traffic to stop before crossing.

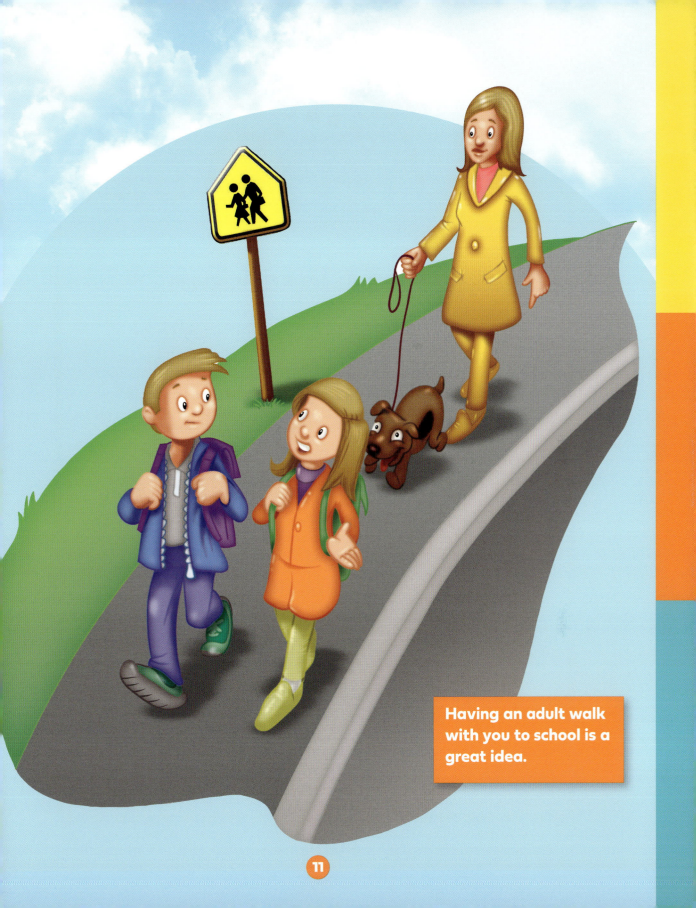

Having an adult walk with you to school is a great idea.

CHAPTER 4

In the Classroom

Your classroom is a pretty safe place to be. But watch out for things that could hurt someone. Keep the floor around your desk clear so your **classmates** won't trip over your things.

Sharp pencils and scissors can poke or seriously hurt someone. Always carry them with the points facing down.

At your desk, sit straight in your chair. Avoid tipping it backward. You could fall and hurt your head.

Telling an adult when you get hurt is important.

If anyone hits or punches you, tell a teacher right away. But what about mean words? Try to work things out on your own first. If someone hurts your feelings, try to stay calm. Say, "I don't like that," and explain why. If you're the one who hurt somebody else's feelings, apologize. Saying you're sorry takes a lot of **courage**, but you can do it.

On the Playground

It's time for recess! Are you ready to play ball and climb the jungle gym? Jungle gyms are fun. But almost half of all injuries on the playground happen on jungle gyms. That's why it's important to stay safe on the jungle gym and the playground.

If you see something that looks sharp or dangerous, stay away from it. Tell an adult who is outside with you. Avoid touching any animals, such as squirrels or birds. Look out for things you could trip over, too.

Broken or sharp items on the playground can be dangerous. Tell an adult right away.

You've climbed up the ladder. Now you are ready to slide! Remember to wait for the person ahead of you to reach the ground before you go. You don't want to crash into someone! And always slide on your bottom, with your feet in front.

Can you go high on the swings? Just be sure to sit on the seat. Wait until the swing stops before you get off. Also, watch out in front and back of the swings so you don't get kicked.

The bell is ringing. School's out! All your classmates are ready to leave. You may be in a hurry, but remember to walk. If you run, you could fall or bump someone else.

Tomorrow will be another day to learn and be safe!

If you see anything—or anyone—**suspicious** at school, always be sure to tell an adult right away!

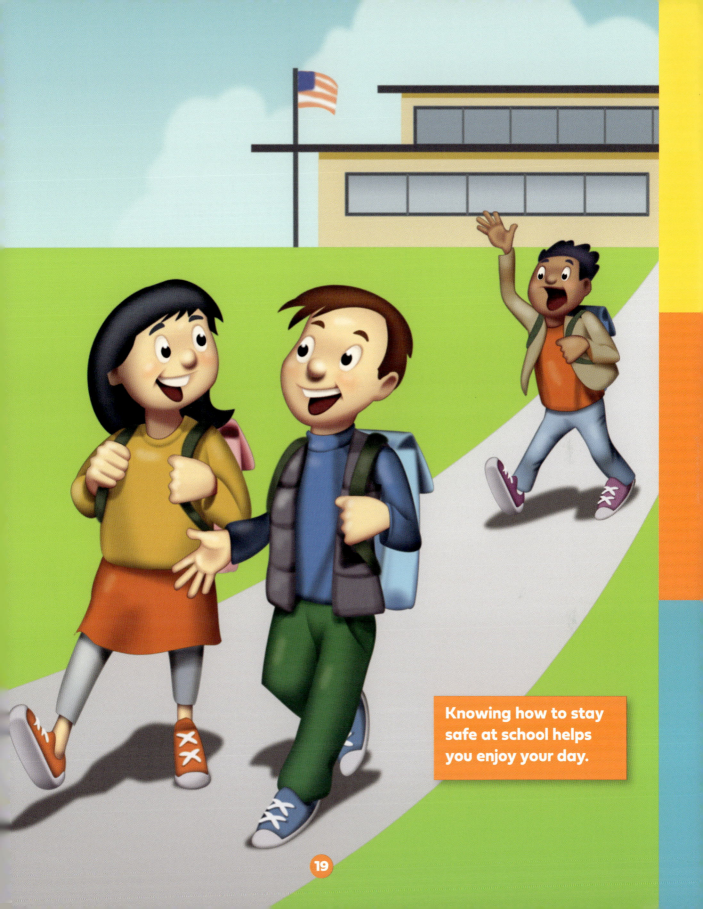

Knowing how to stay safe at school helps you enjoy your day.

School Safety Rules

- Wait at the bus stop with a parent or a friend.

- Make sure your bus driver can always see you when you are outside the bus.

- Sit quietly on the bus and face forward.

- If you walk to school, walk with a friend or a parent.

- Use playground equipment safely.

- Tell an adult if something happens that hurts or scares you.

- Move carefully in the classroom, and don't tip your chair.

- Always walk in school.

Always be safe!

Wonder More

Wondering about New Information

How much did you know about school safety before you read this book? What new information did you learn? Write down three new facts that this book taught you. Was the new information surprising? Why or why not?

Wondering How It Matters

How do drills such as fire drills and lockdown drills help prepare for emergencies? How do you feel when you know your school is safe?

Wondering Why

Why is it important for everyone at school to feel safe? Explain your answer.

Ways to Keep Wondering

After reading this book, what questions do you have about school safety? What can you do to learn more about it?

School Safety Hunt

Search for safety in your school.

You will need:

- A marker, pen, or pencil
- A list of safety items on a piece of paper. Some ideas:
    - exit signs
    - a fire extinguisher
    - a sign with classroom safety rules
    - a crosswalk

Instructions:

Take your list and a marker, pen, or pencil and walk around your school before or after class. See how many things you can check off your safety list. If you see dangerous items, tell an adult right away!

School Safety Hunt

☐ exit signs

☐ fire extinguisher

☐ safety rules sign

☐ crosswalk

Glossary

accident (AK-si-dunt): An accident is something unexpected that happens. In a bus accident, a bus could run into something.

classmates (KLASS-mayts): Classmates are the other children in your class. Be nice to your classmates.

courage (KUR-ij): Courage is bravery. Sometimes it takes courage to apologize.

crosswalk (KROSS-wahk): A crosswalk is a specially marked area on a street where people can cross safely.

distract (diss-TRAKT): To distract someone means to interrupt someone who is focusing on something. Do not distract your bus driver while he or she is driving.

suspicious (sus-PISH-uss): When something is suspicious, it gives you a bad feeling, like something is wrong.

Find Out More

In the Library

Cook, Julia. *I'm Not Scared...I'm Prepared!: A Picture Book to Help Kids Navigate School Safety Threats.* Chattanooga, TN: National Center for Youth Issues, 2014.

Coyle, Becky. *School Bus Safety: An Introduction to Rules and Safety on the School Bus.* Franklin, TN: Flowerpot Press, 2024.

Fitzgerald, Pattie. *Super Duper Safety School: Safety Rules For Kids & Grown-Ups!* Santa Monica, CA: Safely Ever After, 2013.

On the Web

Visit our Web site for links about school safety:

childsworld.com/links

Note to Parents, Teachers, and Librarians: We routinely verify our Web links to make sure they are safe and active sites. So encourage your readers to check them out!

Index

animals, 14

bikes, 10

bus, 4, 6, 7, 8, 9

bus driver, 6, 7, 8, 9

bus stop, 6, 7

crosswalk, 10

desk, 12

feelings, 13

floor, 12

jungle gym, 14

ladder, 16, 17

recess, 4, 14

scissors, 12

scooters, 10

sharp, 12, 14, 15

slide, 16, 17

stairs, 6

swings, 16, 17

walk, 6, 7, 8, 10, 11

weather, 10

window, 8